THE RIGHT CAREER FOR ME

T0356116

COSMETOLOGIST

KATHLEEN A. KLATTE

ROSEN PUBLISHING

Published in 2025 by The Rosen Publishing Group, Inc.
2544 Clinton Street, Buffalo, NY 14224

Portions of this work were originally authored by Sally Ganchy and published as *A Career as a Cosmetologist*. All new material in this edition was authored by Kathleen A. Klatte.

Cover Designer: Michael Flynn
Intertior Designer: Rachel Rising
Editor: Kathleen A. Klatte

Library of Congress Cataloging-in-Publication Data

Names: Klatte, Kathleen A., author.
Title: Cosmetologist / Kathleen A. Klatte.
Description: Buffalo : Rosen Publishing, [2025] | Series: The right career for me | Includes index.
Identifiers: LCCN 2024005338 (print) | LCCN 2024005339 (ebook) | ISBN 9781499476347 (library binding) | ISBN 9781499476330 (paperback) | ISBN 9781499476354 (ebook)
Subjects: LCSH: Beauty operators--Juvenile literature. | Beauty culture--Vocational guidance--Juvenile literature.
Classification: LCC TT958 .K58 2025 (print) | LCC TT958 (ebook) | DDC 646.7/2023--dc23/eng/20240310
LC record available at https://lccn.loc.gov/2024005338
LC ebook record available at https://lccn.loc.gov/2024005339

Some of the images in this book illustrate individuals who are models. The depictions do not imply actual situations or events.

Manufactured in the United States of America

CPSIA Compliance Information: Batch #CSRYA25. For further information, contact Rosen Publishing at 1-800-237-9932.

Find us on

CONTENTS

INTRODUCTION

Some of the oldest-surviving artwork in the world depicts people who have beautified themselves. Ancient Egyptian paintings show people wearing wigs and makeup. Sculptures depict ancient Greeks and Romans with elaborately braided and curled hair. The Greeks treated their hair with scented oils. The Romans used kohl and rouge on their faces. During ancient China's Chou dynasty, royalty painted their fingernails gold and silver. The 18th century, especially in France, was noted for elaborate wigs the upper classes wore. Wigs were curled and pinned into styles, often built up over a wire frame. They were dusted with powder and trimmed with bows, ribbons, and even small sculptures of birds and ships.

Both men and women in ancient Egypt used cosmetics. The characteristic heavy kohl eye makeup also protected their eyes from the sun's glare.

A look like this says a lot about the person wearing it. It's an expression of their personality, but it also says they have the time and money to spend achieving and maintaining this look

Hair and makeup trends change over time, sometimes radically. The ornate fashions and wigs of the 18th century were followed by the Regency era fashions—loose, high-waisted gowns that didn't require corsets or panniers. Hairstyles featured soft buns and loose curls, often modeled on Roman sculptures. This was followed by the more structured fashions of the Romantic and Victorian eras. Despite what you may have heard in the movies, Victorian ladies wore makeup. However, it wasn't respectable to look made up.

People use hair and makeup to show their individual style, social status, or cultural background.

During the 20th century in America, hair and makeup styles reflected the movements transforming society. Each decade there was a reaction against the styles and ideas of the past. In the 1920s, newly liberated women expressed their independence by chopping off their long hair and wearing sleek, Jazz Age bobs. In the 1950s, women celebrated the return to normality after a long war by creating elaborate hairdos that looked natural but were actually held in place with intense styling, usually requiring a weekly trip to the beauty parlor. The hippies of the 1960s and 1970s expressed their longing for a freer and more natural lifestyle by growing their hair long and straight.

Today, how we choose to wear our hair, nails, and makeup continues to reflect our values, aspirations, and preoccupations. Style can make a statement about who you are. Some people prefer a "wash and wear" look that lets them get going quickly and easily. Others prefer a more polished look, or perhaps work in a field where a certain image is required. Looking good can help you project an aura of confidence, competence, and control. Beautiful hair, skin, and nails can make a special day like a wedding or prom even more perfect. They can make an average-looking actor into a star. And who has the power to radically transform appearances? Cosmetologists.

Cosmetologists help people achieve their own unique style.

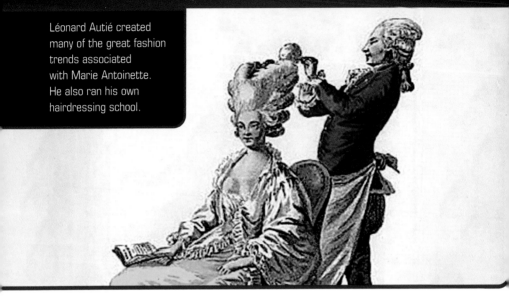

Léonard Autié created many of the great fashion trends associated with Marie Antoinette. He also ran his own hairdressing school.

In ancient Rome, the hairstyles of the rich and famous were achieved by enslaved people called ornatrices. They are often considered the first professional hairdressers. Marie Antoinette had a personal hairdresser named Léonard Autié. Today, cosmetologists are professionals trained in the art of cutting and styling hair, manicuring nails, performing skin treatments, and applying makeup. They may be employed by a salon or spa, or they may go into business for themselves. They may work part time to earn a little extra cash, or they may become fashion moguls who open up chains of salons in all of the world's great cities.

According to the Bureau of Labor Statistics, careers in cosmetology are predicted to grow at a faster rate than other occupations over the next decade. You may recall news stories from the pandemic about how eager people were to be able to return to getting their hair and nails done by professionals. Cosmetology is a broad field with many different career opportunities.

NOT JUST ABOUT GLAMOR

A career in cosmetology doesn't have to be all about glamor. Some cosmetologists work in places such as nursing homes and hospitals. With some patients, especially the elderly, there's a safety aspect—patients might not be steady enough on their feet to stand in the shower and wash their own hair. It's safer for a hairdresser to do it while they're seated. The benefits of having clean hair and a healthy scalp are obvious. However, there's also a mental component to offering beaty treatments to patients—when people look nice, they feel better. This is especially true of cancer patients, whose appearance can be drastically affected by their medical treatments.

Beyond feeling clean and looking nice, patients enjoy the feeling of someone taking care of them.

CHAPTER ONE

WHERE DO I START?

A career in cosmetology requires more than a love of beauty. It requires certain skills and personality traits. You need to be creative, but also organized and disciplined. That might sound like a contradiction, but unrestrained creativity usually results in a mess. When someone goes to a hairdresser or makeup artist, they want them to achieve a particular look—not whatever the heck they feel like doing that day. They want to walk into a clean, organized space and feel confident they're in the hands of a competent professional.

DO YOU HAVE THE RIGHT STUFF?

Cosmetologists need to be friendly and outgoing. In fact, building relationships with clients is an important part of growing your business. In particular, elderly clients might not get out to many different places. Their weekly trip to get their hair done might be the highlight of their week. If your clients enjoy your company, they'll be more likely to use your services again. You must be enthusiastic, outgoing, friendly, compassionate, diplomatic, and energetic. Sometimes, you may be called upon to gently explain to a client why their favorite star's latest look won't work for them.

Cosmetology is a creative field. If you excel at sculpture, painting, design, or other arts, you'll find that those skills will serve you well as a cosmetologist. For instance, hairdressers need the eye of a sculptor as they cut and shape hair. Colorists and makeup artists need a painter's understanding of color. This theoretical artistic knowledge needs to be adapted to working with real people's skin and hair.

Professional makeup artists must understand how colors work together, how colors work with different skin tones, and how those colors will look under different types of lighting.

It's also important to have an interest in fashion. Clients often rely on their hairstylists to keep their look updated. They might ask makeup artists to provide fresh makeup ideas for special events. Sometimes this requires special knowledge, such as what makeup palette works best on a bride or debutante, so their white gown doesn't make them look washed out.

A cosmetologist must be clean and organized. You and your tools will be touching people's hair and skin. You must be willing to work quickly and efficiently so you don't waste time during an appointment. You should be a self-starter, especially if you hope to have your own business someday.

CHOOSING A PROGRAM

There are a variety of ways you can train for a career in cosmetology. You need to consider your career goals and what you can reasonably afford.

There are vocational high schools across the country where students can start their cosmetology training before they get their high school diploma. However, these students will still need to complete some training after high school and earn a cosmetology license before going to work as a cosmetologist.

It's also possible to train as a cosmetologist at a college or university. In a college setting, you can learn cosmetology while taking advantage of a wider variety of educational opportunities. You can also take business classes, which will be useful if you'd like to work as an independent contractor or open your own shop someday. Colleges and universities may also offer more options for financial aid.

The most common route to becoming a cosmetologist is to enroll in cosmetology school, which is also known as beauty school. There are a range of schools at different price points. If your ultimate goal is to work in high fashion or film, it might be worth the investment to attend a prestigious school in New York or California. In many states, you must have graduated from high school or earned a General Educational Development (GED) diploma to go to cosmetology school. Check the requirements in your state.

Some students opt to go to a school that covers only their specific area of interest. Therefore, you may hear aspiring beauty professionals talk about going to nail school, aesthetician school, hair school, barbering school, electrolysis school, or makeup school. However, if you can afford it, a full cosmetology program will give you more options for your future.

COSMETOLOGY SCHOOL

Cosmetology schools and beauty schools teach students the science and theory behind cosmetology and the basic techniques for beautifying and caring for hair, nails, and skin. At any cosmetology school, you'll have a textbook to introduce basic concepts and skills. The two most common texts are from Pivot Point or Milady. You'll take tests, just like in high school. Many beauty schools have an in-school salon for students to practice their new skills.

In addition to art classes, you'll also want a solid background in high school science. It's helpful to know the biology of how nails, skin, and hair grow and how they become damaged or diseased. Cosmetology programs also teach chemistry so that you understand how the products you use will work on your clients. It's also important to know the hazards of some of the chemicals that you will be working with as a cosmetologist. Chemistry will help you understand why certain treatments can't be performed at the same time.

In cosmetology school, you'll learn how to style hair like a professional, from salon shampooing techniques to strategies for sculpting every type of hair. It's standard now for most accredited programs to include ethnic and African American hair. You'll practice executing all the classic haircuts. You'll also learn the art of hairdressing, executing hairstyles such as updos and French braids. Then there are hair treatments meant to change the texture or color of hair. You'll color and dye hair, create highlights, perform permanent waves, and straighten curly hair. In cosmetology school, you will also learn about nails. You'll give manicures and pedicures and discuss how to choose proper nail treatments. You might opt to receive some advanced training in preparing and applying acrylic nails.

A comprehensive cosmetology education also includes an introduction to aesthetics. In this area, you'll learn about the proper care of the skin. You'll learn how to give facials and how to safely remove unwanted body and facial hair. You'll also master makeup, from the basics to advanced techniques such as applying fake eyelashes.

A brand name salon school such as Paul Mitchell or Aveda costs considerably more than many other options. However, if you dream of working in high fashion, it might be a worthwhile investment.

Many cosmetology schools allow students to pick an area of focus. While it's important to get a strong overall education in cosmetology, it's also important to know your strengths and pursue a specialty.

Any beauty school accredited by the National Accrediting Commission of Career Arts and Sciences (NACCAS) will provide a solid education. Unless you have your heart set on a high-end glamor career, you can probably get the education you need at a local beauty school or community college.

WHAT'S MY INVESTMENT?

There are many factors involved in determining how long your training will take and how much it will cost. If you live in Arizona and want to become an aesthetician, you will need to complete 600 hours of training and practice. You can get your license in that area alone. However, if you want to be licensed as a full cosmetologist, you will need 1,600 hours of experience to get your license.

Where you live is also a consideration. In New York, a cosmetologist needs 1,000 hours of training; in Idaho, 2,000 hours of training or 4,000 hours of apprenticeship are required for a cosmetology license. The process of going through cosmetology school will be longer in a state where the licensing rules require more practice hours. And if the schooling is longer, it will likely be more expensive. The average cosmetology program in the United States takes less than 2,000 hours to complete.

If you train at a local beauty school or community college, you remove travel costs and room and board from the financial equation. You also need to consider what's included in your program. For example, a program that includes your toolkit might ultimately cost less than having to buy a kit on your own. It will definitely save you time.

THINGS TO CONSIDER

There are lots of things to think about when choosing a beauty school.

First, consider location. Where do you want to study cosmetology? If you want to stay close to home, it makes sense to look for a beauty school nearby. Remember, there are opportunities in the cosmetology industry everywhere. Not everyone dreams of having their work featured on the cover of *Vogue*. Your goal may be to open a beauty parlor on Main Street.

There's more to choosing a school than just location. You'll need to do more research, asking many questions about each program. What classes does the school offer? If you have a particular specialty in mind you may need to travel to find it. Do the students practice only on mannequin heads, or can they practice on real clients in an in-school salon? Can students take advanced courses in your preferred field of study?

What are the school's hours? If the school offers night and weekend classes, it may make it easier to practice with real, live clients or work while you go to school. How long is the program? Do students have to attend full time, or can they go to school part time?

It is also a good idea to find out how successful the school is at transitioning students into the working world. Does the school offer assistance with job placement after school? What percentage of the school's graduates find work in their fields? And where do they work? If your goal is to work on movie sets, you'd better look for a school with lots of graduates in the film industry.

Many students feel it's important to go to an accredited beauty school. If a cosmetology school is accredited, it can give government financial aid to its students.

To answer these questions, read the school's materials and ask questions of school representatives. Visiting the campus can help you decide whether the school is right for you. When you're on campus, you can see the teaching style of the instructors and watch how the students interact with each other. Even during training, are the workstations neat and organized? Does everything look clean and sanitary? Do you feel comfortable at the school? Do you feel inspired? Try talking to current students. What do they see as the school's strong and weak points?

Will you do all your training on mannequins? Or will you work on fellow students? Will you work on paying customers during your training?

HOW MUCH WILL IT COST?

Perhaps one of the things that drew you to a trade like cosmetology is that a traditional four-year college is out of reach financially. This is a legitimate concern. Cosmetology school is generally less expensive than many colleges and universities but is still an investment. Before you apply to beauty school, consider whether you can afford it. Will the school be able to help you with grants or loans? If not, can you go to school part time so you can put yourself through school by working? Does the school offer work-study programs?

Many students hope to spend as little time and money as possible on their education. But remember, you can't fake skill and confidence in the salon. If you have a solid education, it will show in your work. Well-educated cosmetologists can work more efficiently and produce better results for their clients. In addition, well-trained cosmetologists have a strong understanding of health and safety. This can help them to work safely in a public health crisis, such as the recent COVID-19 pandemic. As a result, cosmetologists who graduate from accredited programs have better job opportunities.

THE COSMETOLOGIST'S TOOLKIT

Cosmetology school is hands on, so you'll need a professional toolkit. Assembling a toolkit on your own can cost thousands of dollars, so the first thing you want to check is if your education program includes a kit. You'll still be paying for it, but it's helpful to know if it's already been included in your tuition and fees. If you need to assemble your own kit, be sure to use a checklist from your school so you get everything you'll need for your classes. Here are some of the standard items you'll need:

Hair: hairstyling tools, including combs, various styling brushes, smocks, shampoo cape, sectioning clips, styling shears, thinning shears, cutting shears, blow-dryer, rollers, curling iron, permanent wave rods, shaving razor, rubber gloves, and a mannequin head with real hair (for practice)

Nails: manicure kit, including nail clippers, cuticle nippers, cuticle pushers, files, buffers, nail brush, bowl, and in some cases even a flexible practice hand

Makeup: full makeup kit, including tweezers, eyelash curlers, applicator wedges, and a wide array of cosmetics

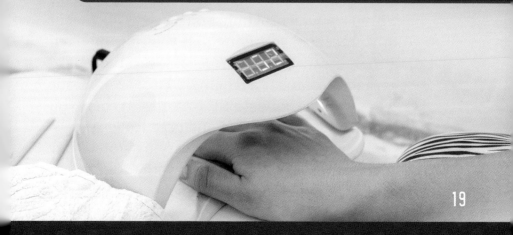

Cosmetology students will learn how to use all sorts of manicure equipment safely, such as this lamp for setting gel manicures.

When considering what you can afford for school, think about where you'd like to work, and how high the cost of living is.

On the other hand, students who start their careers deep in debt face a big challenge. No one goes from the classroom directly to backstage at Fashion Week or owning their own salon. In the first few years of your career, when you're still building a client base, you will probably struggle to make ends meet. This will be even more difficult if you must make big student loan payments. You will need to decide the right balance between the cost of your education and its quality. Remember, this is an investment in the rest of your professional life.

GETTING YOUR LICENSE

Once you complete your training program, you're still not quite ready to work. You still need to pass a licensing exam. In New York, you must be at least 17 years old and have completed a 1,000-hour approved training program. You'll need a document from your school certifying that you've completed the program satisfactorily. You'll also need a medical exam, and to complete a required course on domestic violence and sexual assault awareness. Then you need to pass both a written and practical exam.

Licensing requirements vary by state. Your school should be able to assist you with the licensing process. There are also test prep books available.

LISTENING SKILLS

Cosmetology is a "people" profession. Listening skills are almost as important as learning to cut hair correctly. Suppose you have a client who would look spectacular with aquamarine hair. Before you get them too invested in the idea, you might want to ask what they do for a living. A lawyer or someone who works in a corporate setting might need to present a conservative image at work. Someone who works outside all day might risk too much sun fading their color or turning it an unwelcome shade.

You especially want to listen to older clients. Often, elderly people are on prescription blood thinners because of heart conditions. This means they can bleed excessively from even a small cut. Gentlemen on blood thinners often wear beards so they don't have to shave and risk nicking themselves. People with diabetes can take a long time to heal. While you should be careful with all your clients, by talking to them, you'll know when you need to be extra cautious.

By getting to know your client, you can help them choose a look that's not only flattering but works for their lifestyle.

21

CHAPTER TWO
ALL ABOUT HAIR

Perhaps the most familiar cosmetology professional is the hairdresser. Most towns have at least one beauty parlor and a barber shop. Hair styling offers a wide range of career possibilities. In a neighborhood shop, you'll work with everyone from kids getting their first haircut to grannies coming in for their weekly 'do. You'll do everything from basic back to school haircuts to updos for weddings and proms. Of course, some of these can be the basis of a specialty business, particularly special events such as weddings.

Hairdressing is perhaps the most demanding and difficult of the subjects in cosmetology school. Here is a taste of what a professional hairdresser is expected to know.

THE BIOLOGY OF HAIR

Good hairdressers need to understand the science of hair. During your cosmetology training, you will learn all about the anatomy of hair. In fact, Milady's curriculum features seven chapters of health and science. Students learn this material before they start on the creative aspects of their training. As a cosmetology student, you'll study the natural life cycle of hair—how hair grows and how it stops growing, falls out, and is replaced by new hair. You will discover what makes straight hair lay flat and curly hair curl. This might sound academic—until you consider that as a hairdresser, you will often be asked to put volume and curl into straight, fine hair or to make curly locks sit perfectly flat. You will likely get a basic grounding in chemistry so that you can recognize which commonly used hairdressing chemicals are useful for treating hair problems or achieving certain styling results. You will also be trained to spot medical conditions, such as dandruff and psoriasis, as well as infectious diseases and pests, such as head lice and scabies. Although hairstylists aren't medical professionals, they do know what a healthy scalp looks like and might point out suspicious moles or scabs their clients might not be able to see for themselves but should have examined. Milady's students study additional "foundation" topics on health, infection control, and chemical safety.

Your new scientific knowledge will help you answer clients' questions. It will help you plan your haircuts to look better even as they grow out. And it will allow you to design cuts to cover bald patches,

Hairdressers need to master a variety of techniques for curling hair.

disguise thinning hair, or avoid strange growth patterns such as cowlicks.

Since you'll be touching clients' scalps all day, cutting their hair, and perhaps sometimes even nicking their skin, you will learn to maintain a professional standard of hygiene. Your beauty school should teach you to disinfect your tools (scissors, brushes, combs, clips, etc.) and your work area after each client. It should emphasize the importance of keeping capes and towels freshly laundered. If you fail to maintain a high standard of cleanliness, you will run the risk of spreading infectious diseases. This training is especially important in the aftermath of the COVID-19 pandemic.

HEALTHY HAIR

Cosmetology school will introduce you to the basics of hair care for all different hair types, from fine to thick, from straight to curly, from oily to dry. You'll learn which products can balance out an oily scalp, moisturize dry hair, and strengthen damaged hair. Today, professional cosmetology schools prepare students to care for all hair types, including ethnic and African American hair.

Cosmetologists perform hair care tasks differently than untrained people do at home. There's a professional way to perform a shampoo in order to relax the hair, get rid of any tangles, massage the scalp, and prepare the entire head for a cut. There's a professional way to comb, brush, blow-dry, curl, and flat iron.

Speaking of damage, you will also learn how to spot hair that's been damaged by too much sun, clumsy or hasty styling, or excessive treatment. It's very important that you recognize damaged hair so you can treat it gently as you cut and style it. You may need to ask questions to figure out what's causing the damage and explain how to avoid it in the future. Problems might include not rinsing salt or chlorine from the hair after swimming or having too many different treatments too close together.

You may need to gently explain that some treatments are best left to professionals, as well as help correct the damage.

DESIGN

All great haircuts start with a great design. Although cosmetology classes will focus on hair and facial structure, taking any art or design classes offered in high school can give you a head start with this concept. Studying hair design can help you plan your haircuts to complement different facial shapes, balance facial features, and help clients mask imperfections. For instance, oblong faces can be softened with short haircuts that kick out, or with

KNOWING WHEN TO SAY "NO"

One very important part of designing a haircut is speaking with the client. Sometimes, this can include telling them "no."

Sometimes a client may want to make a change that is impossible, considering his or her hair thickness, movement, or texture. Sometimes a client may request a change of texture that you believe will not be flattering. In cases such as these, you need to be able to explain your concerns tactfully. In addition, it's important you learn to recognize damaged hair. If a client with seriously fried hair asks you to perform a chemical treatment such as a perm or relaxer, you will need to refuse and explain why, in addition to correcting the damage.

A client may come in with a photo of their favorite star's latest look. You may need to explain that the style is expensive to achieve, or perhaps needs a great deal of daily attention to maintain. After all, movie stars are prepped for photos by an entire staff, which most people don't have access to on a daily basis. Knowing how to communicate with a client in an honest yet positive way is one of the cosmetologist's most important skills.

Understanding your client's lifestyle is key to helping them develop a great look. Do they swim every day? Participate in a sport that requires a helmet? Do they shower or wash their hair multiple times a day?

layered looks. If a client has a round face, you can lengthen it with long hair. You'll learn what types of cuts work best for thick hair, fine hair, limp hair, tightly curled hair, and everything in between.

Once you know the theory behind which cuts look great on which faces, you can customize your cuts for the lucky person sitting in your salon chair. You can start to approach your work not just as a hairdresser, but also as an artist. Of course, you still need to adapt your artistry for the client's lifestyle and personal abilities.

CUTTING AND STYLING

Contemplating cutting someone's hair can be scary. What if you mess up? What if they hate it? In beauty school, you'll learn to cut with confidence. You'll learn how to use facial features as guides to keep your haircut symmetrical and balanced. You'll practice sectioning the hair before you cut it. And you will discover strategies for dealing with surprising hair growth patterns such as bald spots and cowlicks.

After you're trained to execute simple hairstyles such as classic bobs, you'll learn advanced cutting techniques such as notching, slicing, thinning, and chunking to create trendy and complicated, sometimes asymmetrical, styles. Your finishing touches are the key to creating sleek, sharp cuts; soft, feathery looks; and even chunky and funky styles.

After the client's hair is cut, it needs to be styled. Clients need the personalized attention of the stylist so they can see the full potential of their new look. You'll become a master stylist, using a hair dryer and brush to create volume or tame unruly

In the past, hairdressers and barbers had to go to special schools to learn how to care for ethnic or African American hair. Today, cosmetology programs covers proper care for all hair types.

and wild hair. You'll use irons to create curls or erase them. You'll be able to confidently pick styling products to recommend to customers so that they can recreate their new look at home. Again, this is where you'll want to consult with your client about how much time and effort they plan to expend on their hair every day.

You may also learn how to care for wigs. This is an essential skill if you'd like to work in movies, television, or theater.

NATURAL ETHNIC AND AFRICAN AMERICAN HAIR

One hundred years ago, beauty schools and salons tended to be segregated, either by law or simply because of the way people tend to congregate in neighborhoods. Pioneering African American cosmetologists such as Madam C.J. Walker, Marjorie Stewart Joyner, and Annie Turnbo Malone created beauty schools and products designed for Black women, but mainstream beauty schools at the time only taught how to care for Caucasian hair.

Today Milady and Pivot Point include training and products for African American hair, as well as Caucasian. While you may wish to take additional training and specialize in different textures and kinds of hair, a solid professional training program will cover the main points. Everyone should feel confident when walking into a salon that hairdressers are trained to care for their type of hair.

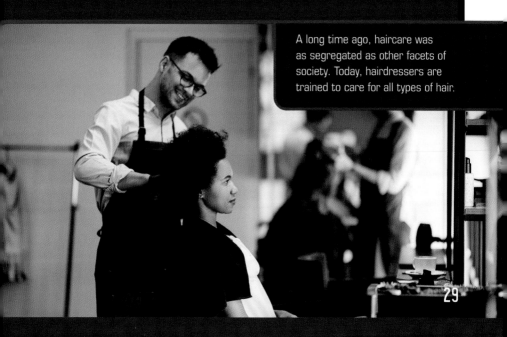

A long time ago, haircare was as segregated as other facets of society. Today, hairdressers are trained to care for all types of hair.

A look like this can be flattering and a great deal of fun! Part of your job will be explaining what's needed to maintain the look.

COLORING

One of the most popular salon treatments is hair coloring. Clients might want to cover up gray hair or brighten a natural color that's darkened with age. They might want to correct for color changes that happened after a salon disaster, overtreatment, or other damage. Or perhaps they want to have fun with a bright new look.

You'll learn about how to recognize clients' true hair color and respect and work with the natural coloring of their skin. You might need to practice your diplomacy and explain why a certain color might not work well with a client's complexion. You'll understand the differences among various hair shades and hair tones. You'll study how to mix colors and identify how long each color takes to "develop" once it's applied to the hair. You will practice a variety of methods for applying color to a client's hair. By the end of beauty school, you should know how to tint hair, highlight it, lowlight it, or change its color completely. You'll also understand how the chemicals in hair color interact with other treatments such as perms.

TEXTURING

Another reason clients visit the salon is because they don't like the texture of their hair. Changing a client's hair texture is one of the more difficult tasks a hairdresser faces. Perhaps it's too limp or thin and needs a lot of product just to hold a simple style. Or maybe it's too thick and curly to easily comb.

Cosmetology school will teach you how to perform a permanent wave, or "perm," to change a client's hair from straight to curly. The process includes treating the client's hair with chemicals and heat. You'll also be initiated into the secrets of relaxing curly hair and making it straight. You may even study specialized treatments, learning to give your clients Brazilian blowouts or Japanese thermal hair straightening.

Of course, after completing the treatment and giving the client their new look, you'll need to explain how to properly care for it. The client may need to wash their hair more or less than they did before and use certain shampoos or conditioners to prolong their look. They may need to learn to use a pick or wide-tooth comb instead of a regular brush. And they'll need to know how long they should wait before doing anything else to their hair.

SAFETY IN THE SALON

One of the less glamorous aspects of cosmetology is learning to practice safety and good hygiene. Hair color, permanent wave solution, and relaxers all contain strong chemicals. Used correctly, they can achieve terrific results. Used carelessly, they can cause allergic reactions or chemical burns. Aside from knowing how to use these materials safely on clients, you must learn how they'll affect you. A client might be breathing in fumes only for the duration of their treatment, but you might perform several treatments in one day, not to mention whatever the cosmetologist next to you is working on.

It's your responsibility to keep yourself educated about the health risks in your workplace. Read the labels of the products you work with, and always follow the safety instructions. If you're working with strong chemicals, wear plastic gloves. Whether you're a hairdresser performing a chemical treatment or a nail tech filing off acrylic nails, make sure that you work in a well-ventilated area and, if necessary, wear a mask. If you are worried about the chemicals used in your workplace, contact your supervisor, and ask if you can switch to a safer substance.

Milady's curriculum includes sections on health and safety. In addition to learning about the different chemicals you'll be working with, you'll also be using electricity and water in close quarters. When hairdryers, curling irons, and other electric equipment are not in use, keep them unplugged so no one trips on the cords. You'll also learn to keep your work area and tools sterilized to minimize infections and pests. And of course, use common sense—mop up all spills and sweep up hair clippings to prevent falls.

Hair or spills on the floor look terrible to a client walking through the salon door. It's also an accident waiting to happen. A good hairdresser cleans up between each client and right away if a mess poses a hazard.

CHAPTER THREE

ALL ABOUT ESTHETICS

Aesthetics is the art and science of maintaining and beautifying skin. It's one of the fastest-growing subfields of cosmetology. There's so much to learn. Scientists and cosmetologists are constantly working together to create new cutting-edge techniques to rejuvenate and beautify the skin. Before studying these exciting new procedures, you need to learn the basics.

The terms "esthetician," "aesthetician," and "licensed skincare specialist" are sometimes used interchangeably. According to the Louisville Beauty Academy, "esthetician" is used for skincare professionals who pursue advanced training for a salon setting. "Aesthetician" is used for skincare professionals who pursue advanced training for a medical setting. However, they first need to complete a standard cosmetology program and get their license.

THE BIOLOGY OF SKIN

You're probably very familiar with pores, particularly how they can become clogged and form blemishes.

And you've probably heard lots about ultraviolet (UV) rays and how to protect your skin from them. But what about collagen? Alpha hydroxy? Hyperpigmentation? You probably know that each of these terms is related in some way to the skin. But could you define them all? If you choose a career as an esthetician, you must be able to understand and use these terms, and hundreds of others, at a moment's notice.

An esthetician can help a client sort through the bewildering and often expensive variety of skin care products on the market.

35

The esthetics curriculum begins with the study of the anatomy of skin. The skin is the body's largest organ. It covers the muscles, internal organs, and bones, and it protects us from pollution, injury, and infection. Skin's ability to heal is incredible. However, it's not limitless. The things we do in life take a toll. Improperly treated acne can leave scars. And one severe sunburn can lead to skin cancer.

The hair and nails are outgrowths of the skin. Hair and nails, however, consist of dead cells. Skin, in contrast, is living. Therefore, the skin can give us an important overall indication of a person's health. When people drink enough water, eat a balanced diet, exercise, and generally take care of themselves, their skin usually looks good. If they don't get enough sleep, are constantly dehydrated, or overindulge in alcohol, cigarettes, or drugs, this tends to take a toll on their skin. Unhealthy living ages the skin prematurely. So does too much sun.

CARING FOR SKIN

Everything you do shows in your skin eventually. However, even the healthiest people need to take good care of their skin to keep it young and fresh looking. Many people don't realize just how seriously the sun's UV rays can damage their skin. This includes skin people don't always think about, such as their scalp. Others have never given much thought to keeping their skin moisturized or hydrated.

An esthetician can identify whether a client's skin is oily or dry, sun damaged or dehydrated. After making an assessment, the esthetician recommends how the client might best improve their skin. Should they get a facial treatment? Or perhaps change their diet or vitamin regimen? What about something simple, such as drinking extra water every day? The esthetician can craft a plan of action to help clients improve their skin.

Estheticians must educate their clients about how to use diet and lifestyle to keep their skin looking good. They share tips with clients about how to use sunscreen, moisturizer, and other products to protect and preserve the skin. And they can plan and perform a course of facial treatments.

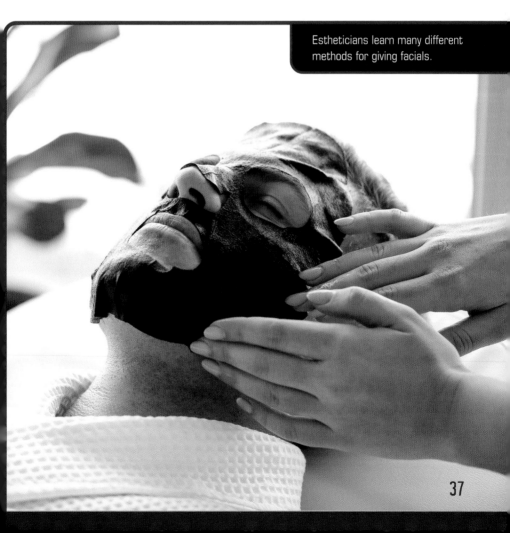

Estheticians learn many different methods for giving facials.

HYGIENE

Although estheticians aren't medical professionals, they're trained to recognize various skin disorders. If you treat someone with a serious skin condition inappropriately, you may harm them. Moreover, if you treat a client with an infectious skin disease, you could spread that disease to other clients—or even catch it yourself.

However, not every disease is visible. That's why it's important that every esthetician maintain a sanitary, sterile work environment. The people who give the esthetics licensing exam observe carefully to make sure that candidates use sterilized equipment and that they know how to keep their work areas pleasant, clean, and safe. Milady covers these topics in both its general cosmetology and esthetics curriculums.

FACIALS

One of the most satisfying and creative parts of being an esthetician is giving facial treatments. A facial typically includes removing the client's makeup, cleansing and toning the skin, and perhaps applying eye cream, massage cream, or other products. The esthetician might also massage the face, scalp, and shoulders to stimulate blood circulation.

Other parts of a facial will vary from client to client. Exfoliating scrubs help clear away the very top layer of the skin, which is generally made up of dead cells, and reveal the healthy, vital cells beneath. This is an instance where the esthetician needs to be especially aware of the ingredients in the products they use. Some creams and cleansers try to copy the effects of a salon treatment by including crystals that scrub the skin. Many products used plastic microbeads for this purpose until they were outlawed in 2015 for causing water pollution. A similar treatment is microdermabrasion. In microdermabrasion, the esthetician uses a special machine to "blast" or sand dead cells off the surface of the face and reveal the younger, glowing skin underneath.

The esthetician may also add a facial steam, pack, or mask. In your cosmetology program, you'll learn how to choose a prepared mask or design and create your own facial mask out of pure ingredients. The point of a facial mask—whether it's made from cucumbers, yogurt, honey, or mud—is to replenish and balance the skin. The same is true for packs, cream masks, and gel masks.

There are so many treatments, techniques, and options for people hoping to improve their skin. The choices are positively dizzying and sometimes pricey. That's why clients are willing to pay to consult with a skin care professional who can help them craft a personalized skin care plan. In addition, many people want to ensure that their cosmetics don't contain any animal products and haven't been tested on animals.

A facial is often part of a relaxing spa day.

HAIR REMOVAL TECHNIQUES

Another issue that brings clients to the salon is unwanted hair. Sometimes this is hair that appears above the upper lip. Other people wish to remove hair from their bikini line. While there are products available for home use, it's often safer and cleaner to go to a professional. Estheticians are often tasked with hair removal through waxing, plucking, or more specialized techniques.

Any hair removal process starts with a client consultation. Some clients should not undergo hair removal. If they have certain allergies, skin disorders, or are taking certain medications, having hair professionally removed may be dangerous to their health.

Estheticians learn how to remove body and facial hair from both men and women. This might be a simple procedure, such as an eyebrow wax. It could involve using tweezers to pluck and shape certain areas or using a depilatory to weaken the hair and make it easier to remove. However, it's important to spot test any kind of chemical to be sure the client won't have an allergic reaction. Whatever the method, you will have to learn to perform the hair removal procedure in the cleanest, most efficient, and least painful way possible. A waxer or other esthetician who can be trusted to keep clean conditions and treat clients with compassion will likely win a lot of return business.

Estheticians may also learn more advanced forms of hair removal. These tend to be more expensive than waxing and tweezing, but they last longer, are cleaner, and in some cases, lead to permanent hair removal. These other methods of hair removal require advanced training and sometimes a separate license. Most states require laser hair removal to be supervised by a doctor, nurse, or physician's assistant. Currently, New York is the only state with no regulations for laser hair removal, although there is a bill in the state senate that will require technicians to be licensed if it passes.

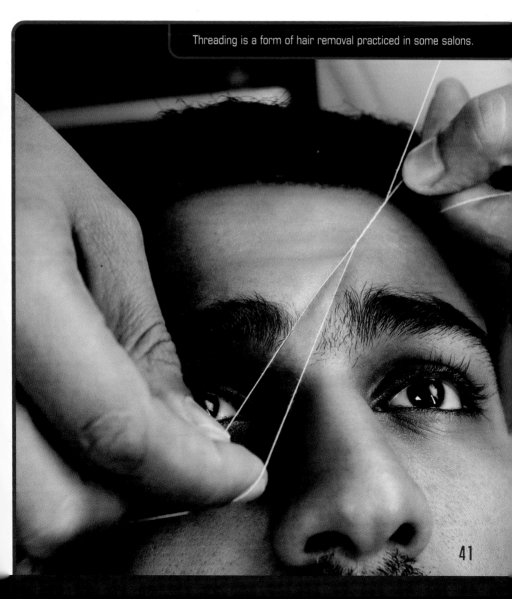
Threading is a form of hair removal practiced in some salons.

41

WHERE DO ESTHETICIANS WORK?

Like traditional cosmetologists, estheticians have a wide range of job opportunities open to them. Some may find employment in a salon or beauty supply retailer. Others might work at a spa, particularly if they have an interest in massage or hydrotherapy, which typically require more space than a salon might offer.

Other places estheticians might work include spas or resorts. Some resorts offer heath-based services, such as fitness and nutrition. Others might offer esthetic services to complement guests' long days spent skiing or at the beach. Cruise ships often have full scale health and wellness facilities. Jobs like these often have fun perks such as discounted winter sports or in the case of a cruise ship, free travel and accommodations.

Resorts and cruise ships that have spa facilities can be the perfect place for an adventurous skin care professional.

Electrolysis is a popular method of permanent hair removal. This method may sound somewhat strange. The esthetician slides an extremely thin metal probe into a hair follicle and zaps it with electricity. The hair is destroyed, and the hope is that after several treatments, the hair follicle will be permanently damaged and will no longer produce hairs. There are many methods of electrolysis, all using different equipment. As an advanced procedure, electrolysis requires its own training. In many states, electrologists must obtain their own special licenses.

Laser hair removal works along the same lines as electrolysis. Instead of inserting metal rods into the hair follicle, the hair follicle is damaged with a laser. Another related hair removal process is photoepilation, which involves intense pulsed light. These treatments can be dangerous if the technician isn't properly trained. Some of the most common complaints are burns, scarring, and discoloration.

Scientists and cosmetologists are always trying to find less painful and more permanent forms of hair removal. Perhaps by the time you study cosmetology, there will be a brand-new "hot" form of hair removal for you to master and offer your clients!

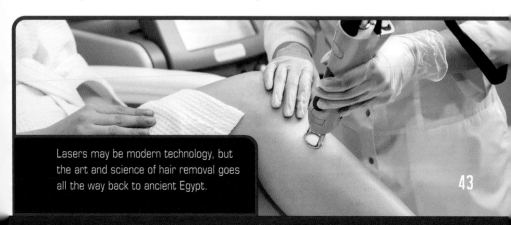

Lasers may be modern technology, but the art and science of hair removal goes all the way back to ancient Egypt.

Makeup artists master all sorts of looks, from the conservative makeup on the TV meteorologist to full-scale glam for prom night.

MAKEUP

Makeup is part of any comprehensive cosmetology course. It may be a fairly small part of the curriculum, but it's probably one of the most fun. You'll begin by learning cosmetic color theory—what colors pair well with various skin tones and hair colors. You'll be trained to use all the major forms of cosmetics, from everyday items such as lipstick and lip gloss to complicated cosmetics such as individual fake eyelashes. Above all, cosmetology school will teach you how to use makeup to emphasize striking features, while downplaying features the client dislikes. This is called corrective makeup.

Some people want an entire career as a makeup artist. There are schools where you can focus on specialty makeup, such as fashion makeup, bridal makeup, and special effects makeup. In small theatrical projects, one person might be responsible for both hair and makeup. In that case, you need the full cosmetology school experience. However, if you plan to work as part of a team, where someone else is responsible for hair, a specialty makeup course

Even if you're not located near a hub of the entertainment industry, there are job opportunities for a trained makeup artist.

might be a better choice for you. If you have a clear vision of your future life as a makeup artist, do your research. Look up people who have the career you want and find out how they got there. Follow in their footsteps.

IATSE

If you want a career in movies or the theater, you'll probably end up joining the International Alliance of Theatrical Stage Employees, Moving Picture Technicians, Artists and Allied Crafts of the United States, Its Territories and Canada (IATSE). This is the union that represents theater technicians—the people behind the scenes who make the magic happen.

Hairstylists and makeup artists work on movies and in theaters. They work on Broadway and for ballet and opera companies. In a large production, there might be a separate staff for hair and another for makeup. In other projects, a single cosmetologist or a small team might provide both hair and makeup. It also depends on the style and setting of the production. A project with a contemporary setting generally requires less time in the chair than fantasy or sci-fi.

Unions such as IATSE negotiate for better pay and safer working conditions for members. In a case such as the recent writers and actors strikes in Hollywood, the union offered emergency aid to members who were out of work because their projects were shut down.

BEFORE

A makeup artist in show business may be called on to make someone look old or sick or like a space alien!

AFTER

CHAPTER FOUR

MARVELOUS MANICURES

One of the biggest components of your cosmetology education is nails. In fact, nails make up the second-largest section of the Milady curriculum. Every beauty school student must spend some time learning about nails. Some students with a real passion for nails may choose to focus their careers in that direction, becoming manicurists, sometimes called nail technicians. Nail technicians are trained to clean, trim, and polish fingernails and toenails. Some skilled nail techs create nail extensions and fake nails. Many enhance their clients' experiences by providing hand, arm, foot, and leg massages.

A comprehensive cosmetology education will come in handy as a nail technician because at some salons, manicurists are also expected to provide hair removal services. The health and safety components of the cosmetology curriculum also come in handy.

Professional manicurists have lots of fun colors and techniques to work with.

ALL ABOUT NAILS

People who work with nails need to know all about them. Manicurists or nail technicians must understand the anatomy and biology of nails. They need to know how nails grow, what makes them weak, what makes them break, and what strengthens them. They should be able to recognize changes in shape or color that indicate something a dermatologist should check out. They should understand the chemistry of the nail so that they will know why certain substances adhere to the nails. This is especially important for nail technicians, since they spend so much time painting nails, coating them, or stripping them.

Aside from making a client's nails look pretty, a professional manicurist needs to be able to recognize unhealthy nails that might signal a medical issue.

SAFETY AND HYGIENE

Just as in other areas of cosmetology, it's important to learn about safety and hygiene when working with nails. Some clients may be allergic to your materials, from nail primers and polishes to gel or acrylic tips. Nail techs work with a wide array of chemicals and processes that need to be treated with care. Nail polish and nail polish removers can have strong, unpleasant odors. Filing acrylic nails can produce dust. This is why it's important for the health of nail technicians and clients that manicures and pedicures be performed in well-ventilated areas.

Nail technicians should also know how to spot and deal with common problems, such as the fungal infections that can sometimes develop in the space between a natural nail and the false nail laid down on top of it. Nail techs work with sharp implements, so it's important to sterilize them between clients.

FINGERS AND TOES

Nail techs perform manicures and pedicures. The nail technician follows a number of steps, usually beginning with removing any nail polish the client is already wearing. Next comes exfoliating and moisturizing; trimming or pushing back the cuticles; shaping, buffing, and cleaning the nails; and finally, polishing and drying. The manicure may also include extra services, such as a paraffin wax dip or a massage.

Pedicures follow the same basic procedure as manicures but come with their own set of challenges and rewards. If you're a person who hates looking at and touching feet, becoming a nail tech is definitely not for you! Not only will you have to clean and shape toenails, but you will also have to file off calluses and deal with corns and blisters.

Men's manicures are on the rise as a form of self-care, so you'll learn how to do that as well. There's really no difference between the service for a male or female client, other than a man might prefer clear polish or none at all.

Men are beginning to appreciate the benefits of relaxing while someone cares for their hands and feet.

During cosmetology training, you'll learn how to create different edges on nails using files, emery boards, cuticle knives, electric files, and other tools. You'll learn how to use those tools safely and keep them sanitary. You'll also learn about how different shapes may complement or detract from various hand shapes—and what kinds of manicures will work best for different clients. Just as a wild haircut will detract from a conservative client's life, an easily broken manicure will be totally inappropriate for a client who works with their hands. This is another case where good communication is a must. Someone who needs their nails relatively short still deserves a fabulous look. It's up to you to figure out how to make it work for your client's lifestyle.

NAIL ART AND DESIGN

Colorful nail polish and clever nail art are the fun part of manicures. Some of the nail designs covered in cosmetology programs include full coverage, half moon, hairline, and free edge. In cosmetology school, you will practice giving manicures that are designed to simply augment and perfect the natural look of a hand, as well as manicures that involve acrylic tips and bright colors or patterns. Again, it's all about the client—their personality, their job, and the reason for today's visit.

Today, there are so many ways for clients to make a fashion statement with their nails. They might express themselves with their favorite colors, glitter, or artwork from their favorite fandom. Many manicurists enjoy creating fun nail designs or using nail wraps that allow them to apply complex pictures and patterns to nails, much like pasting over a billboard.

An amazing manicure like this might be the perfect finishing touch for a bride.

ARTIFICIAL NAILS AND NAIL ENHANCEMENTS

Cosmetology school teaches students how to do the demanding work of creating nail tips and extensions. These "fake nails" are much more complicated and demanding than the press-ons sold at your local drug store. As a nail technician, your clients will look to you to create strong, natural-looking, and fashionable nails. Some of the nail extension technologies you might be called upon to use include silk, fiberglass, or linen wraps; acrylic tips; and gel nails.

53

Wraps are used to add strength and length to the nail. This can be done with silk, which is flexible, lightweight, and natural; linen, which is strong and thick and can be more noticeable than silk; and fiberglass, which can be both strong and flexible. These wraps are especially useful if the natural nail underneath a tip or extension has been damaged and must be protected.

Nail technicians also use acrylic nails to add length. First, artificial tips are added onto the nail. Next, the nail and tip together are covered with a layer of acrylic. Acrylic nails must be filed and shaped. These nails are formed chemically, so they must be removed very carefully so that the natural nail isn't damaged.

BRIDAL COSMETOLOGY

Even the most casual people want to look good on their wedding day. After all, they paid a lot of money for an expensive gown, and even more money for a photographer to record the event. A common trend today is for a cosmetologist, or a team to go to the bride's home or hotel—wherever the bridal party is dressing—instead of the bride visiting the salon.

Some hairdressers and makeup artists specialize in bridal hair and makeup. Many women decide that on their wedding day, they want a more elaborate hairstyle or a special look that will complement their dress. They may also want their party to have complementary hairstyles. Those who specialize in bridal hair and makeup need to know how to execute elaborate hairstyles, especially those that can accommodate a veil, flowers, or other hair ornaments. Bridal makeup artists should be able to work quickly but meticulously under pressure. They need to know which products will keep a bride from looking washed out from her white gown and veil. They'll also use products that can hold up to tears and not smudge. The bride wants to look good for all of what can be a very long day.

Promptness and responsibility are absolute musts! A wedding day is usually timed to the minute for getting people to different venues. Anyone working with brides should be diplomatic, calming, and kind. Many cosmetologists who choose this field enjoy working with clients during one of life's happiest events.

A bride not only needs to look lovely, but she also needs to know that her makeup won't smudge off all over the people she's hugging and kissing all day!

Gel nails are similar in many ways to acrylic nails. Gel nail polish is applied from a bottle like regular nail polish. Then it's hardened under a UV light. While acrylic nails have a strong odor, gel nails have the advantage of being almost odorless. Gel nails last about two weeks and can be carefully removed using regular acetone nail polish remover.

Acrylic nails need to be filled regularly. As the natural nail grows out, it pushes the artificial nail away from the cuticle, leaving a gap between the skin and the artificial nail. A nail technician can "fill in" the gap with more acrylic. This extends the life of the original manicure.

Nail techs also need to educate clients about how to care for their artificial nails. Some people believe that wraps and similar treatments aren't good for their nails, but many problems occur because clients try to remove wraps and tips themselves incorrectly.

NAIL TECHNOLOGY SCHOOL

Students who know that they want to focus exclusively on nail technology may decide to skip cosmetology or beauty school and go straight to nail tech school. It's possible to obtain a license to do nails only, and the amount of time required to get this license is much shorter than the overall cosmetologist degree or license sequence. However, nail techs who exclusively give manicures and pedicures tend to make less money than cosmetologists who can offer their clients services in several different areas. Becoming a licensed nail technician gives you exposure to the beauty industry. You'll have a paying job if you decide later on that you'd like to complete a full cosmetology program.

MORTUARY COSMETOLOGY

Mortuary cosmetology is a specialized field. It involves preparing a deceased person for viewing at their wake or funeral. The goal is to make them look as lifelike as possible, so the grieving family has a pleasant final image of their loved one.

This can involve applying makeup and styling the decedent's hair as they normally wore it. In the case of someone's who's been sick for a long time or died in an accident, padding may need to be applied to restore the proper shape of the face.

This is exacting work that must be performed with the utmost regard for safety and sanitation, as well as compassion for the grieving family. This job may be performed by a licensed cosmetologist or a licensed embalmer.

A funeral is a last chance to say goodbye to a loved one. A mortuary cosmetologist can help a family say goodbye with dignity.

CHAPTER FIVE

CHOOSING YOUR PATH

Once you've graduated and gotten your license, your adventure really begins! Hopefully, while you've been training, you've also been thinking about what sort of place you'd like to work in and what aspect of cosmetology you'd like to specialize in. It's probably best to start out in a salon so you can see different cosmetology fields in action, but remember, you're not limited to your local beauty shop and eventually, you might like to choose a specialty.

HAIRDRESSERS AND BARBERS

Many people go to beauty school to become hairdressers. You already know a hairdresser's basic duties: consulting with clients, cutting hair, styling it, and educating clients about how to care for their new cuts. As a hairdresser, you might work in a small-town Supercuts salon giving basic cuts to local families or in a high-fashion urban salon where stylists make big money working with demanding, wealthy clients. You might work in a theater or make weekly visits to local nursing homes. The possibilities are endless.

Although many men are becoming more confident about seeking salon services like manicures, some men still prefer to go to a barbershop. A barber is a professional trained to cut and trim men's hair and care for their facial hair through shaves, trims, and grooming. In fact, many barbers go to special barbering schools.

Some men enjoy salons and spas, others prefer the atmosphere of a barber shop.

MANICURISTS AND NAIL TECHS

Becoming a manicurist or nail tech is another popular choice. This can offer a lot of flexibility. You might work in a salon giving full manicures and pedicures. At more advanced levels, you may lengthen clients' nails using acrylic or gel nails. Or you might do something like visit people in their homes to do their nails.

Some nail techs work in special nail salons that concentrate exclusively on giving manicures and pedicures. Others work in salons and spas that offer a wider array of services. In some salons, the manicurist may offer hair removal services or double as an esthetician. This is where attending a full cosmetology program, instead of one concentrated on nails comes in—you have more flexibility. In tough times, the more skills you have, the better your chances of finding work. Or perhaps you dream of opening your own nail shop.

ESTHETICIANS

Estheticians are skin care specialists. They're often employed by spas or salons to give clients facials, perform body wraps, and design skin care regimens. Estheticians might also be employed by resorts and even cruise ships. They may be trained to remove unwanted facial and body hair for clients. Some are trained in high-tech hair removal techniques, such as electrolysis, laser hair removal, or exotic and lesser-known techniques such as sugaring and threading. A firm grounding in cosmetology is recommended, as the aestheticians at some spas and salons are asked to give manicures and pedicures as well.

Estheticians may also receive special training that qualifies them to offer their clients special services, such as aromatherapy, reflexology, acupuncture, LED light therapy, hydrotherapy, and acupressure. Some of these techniques require additional licensing. As an esthetician, you'll always have something new to learn to offer more value to your clients.

HAIR REMOVAL SPECIALISTS

Some estheticians specialize in hair removal. Electrologists specialize in permanent hair removal through electrolysis. Others focus on laser hair removal. These professionals are sometimes entrepreneurs who run their own businesses and build their own loyal clientele. They may work out of their own establishment or visit the salons and spas of others to practice their trade. Check your local laws to find out what the electrolysis licensing regulations in your state are. Laser hair removal requires special certification in many states. Some places require it to be performed under the supervision of a licensed medical professional. This is another field where you need to be aware of changing laws and how they affect you.

Hair removal requires special training and in some locations, a special license.

PARAMEDICAL AESTHETICIANS

Paramedical aestheticians work in doctors' offices, helping to prepare clients for cosmetic surgery and other medical procedures. They work in a dedicated medical setting, rather than a salon or spa. Paramedical aestheticians might offer other services such as Botox injections, chemical peels, skin care after surgery, and hair removal for clients whose medical situation disqualifies them from seeing a regular esthetician. Paramedical aestheticians also offer clients pre- and post-operative care for facelifts. They might also use makeup to help clients conceal healing skin while recovering from surgery. Educational and licensing requirements can vary by state, so this is a field you want to investigate thoroughly before choosing an educational program.

MASSAGE THERAPISTS

Massage therapy is a fast-growing field that can earn a comfortable living. Massage therapists are often employed by a salon or spa to give clients relaxing and rejuvenating massages as part of a luxurious spa experience. They are also employed at places such as cruise ships or resorts, which can include fun job perks such as discounted recreational amenities.

Massage therapists can also alleviate serious physical pain. Using touch, physical pressure, and manipulations of the muscles through the skin, massage therapists can significantly improve a client's life. Some work in medical facilities such as sports medicine clinics or physical therapy offices.

If you're interested in a career as a massage therapist, forgo cosmetology school and proceed directly to massage school. You'll learn many different techniques, including deep tissue massage, Swedish massage, Japanese shiatsu massage, and sports massage. Generally, massage therapists are required to have a high school diploma before completing an accredited training program and passing a licensing exam. Requirements vary by state but can include a clean background check and a valid cardiopulmonary resuscitation (CPR) certification.

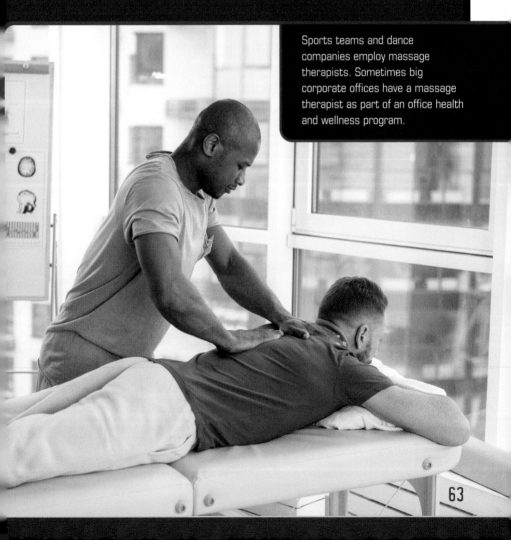

Sports teams and dance companies employ massage therapists. Sometimes big corporate offices have a massage therapist as part of an office health and wellness program.

MAKEUP ARTISTS

Makeup artistry is a career choice with lots of possibilities. Some makeup artists work in cosmetic stores, beauty supply stores, or at cosmetic counters in department stores. There is no special training needed for these jobs. In fact, some beauty professionals recommend that if you are considering a career as a makeup artist, you might want to first get a job at a makeup counter or makeup store. That way, you can see whether the job is truly to your liking before investing in beauty school or makeup school.

As technology makes it easier to document our lives, makeup artists are more in demand than ever to prepare ordinary people for special events such as weddings and proms. Bridal makeup is a lucrative and growing field. Mortuary cosmetology is also very makeup intensive.

At higher levels, skilled makeup artists are in demand to prepare models for fashion shoots and runway shows. You must be extremely well respected and lucky to land these jobs. You also need to work

Working in the fashion industry is very demanding—and very competitive.

well under pressure and have the tact to deal with "big" personalities.

Theater, film, and television productions always need makeup artists. The work in these industries can range from simply making a great-looking star look even better to artificially aging a young person, changing a person's gender, or even creating an outlandish character such as an orc, werewolf, dwarf, or alien. Special effects makeup is extremely specialized and uses all sorts of advanced techniques such as airbrushing and latex application. Anybody who is serious about going into this field needs to be well trained. Aside from the creative aspect of the job, special effects makeup artists also need to be concerned about being kind to the actor's skin. Some special effects makeup artists attend special schools, while others apprentice with an established special effects makeup artist. Halloween events, permanent haunted attractions, and theme parks employ makeup artists, too.

PERMANENT MAKEUP

Permanent makeup or micropigmentation refers to the practice of tattooing designs that imitate makeup onto a client—for instance, applying lines on the eyelids that look like eyeliner or eye shadow. This field combines the skills of the makeup artist and the tattoo artist. Permanent makeup is classified with tattooing and body piercing for licensing and regulatory purposes. The demand for these services varies greatly from region to region. Research the demand for permanent makeup artists in your area before you commit to a course of study.

COLOR OR TEXTURE SPECIALIST

Large salons might employ a hair texture specialist who is responsible for taking on challenging texture jobs and staying informed about the latest hair texture procedures, techniques, and products. This specialist may also train other hairdressers in the salon to use new texture processes and products. Salons sometimes employ a hair color specialist, whose job is to perform expert highlights, lowlights, tints, and dye jobs. This colorist might also train fellow hairdressers in color application. This can be helpful as there are always brand-new color products on the market.

SALON MANAGERS

A salon is a business that needs a manager to keep it running in an efficient and professional manner. The manager's job is to hire, train, and schedule employees. He or she also hires receptionists, janitors, and other staff. Managers order beauty supplies and ensure the salon's equipment is in working order. Above all, the salon manager sees that the salon is running smoothly and that customers are happy.

Managing a salon isn't a job that you get straight out of beauty school. In general, managers start out as hair stylists or estheticians. They learn about the creative side of the trade, get a little experience, and see how the salon works. After that, they may be able to take on more managerial responsibility. Some beauty programs include business basics. Or if this is something that interests you, you might consider taking business classes at a community college.

SALON OR SPA OWNERS

Perhaps you dream of owning your own salon or spa. This is something that takes time and planning. You might buy an existing salon so you don't need to choose a location, buy fixtures, or build a clientele. Or you might build an entirely new salon from the ground up to suit your own personal vision.

As the owner of a salon or spa, you must be aware of every detail of the business. Before attempting to be an owner, you should have already mastered all of the skills of the salon manager. Besides this, you must also deal with paying rent, paying employees, marketing the salon, attracting customers, and all sorts of legal issues, such as permits and insurance. You must have a vision for your business so that you can create a plan of action that will make your dream a reality. This is a difficult career path, but the rewards can be tremendous.

Today, every business needs someone dedicated to managing its social media accounts.

Because there is so much involved in starting a successful business (or even buying an existing business and keeping it successful), many salon owners decide to study business at the college or graduate level. An owner will spend much more time in the office than working in the salon. This is something to consider if you really enjoy practicing cosmetology.

BEAUTY SUPPLY STORE OWNERS AND MANAGERS

Not all beauty careers involve a salon! One interesting alternative is a beauty supply store, where professional cosmetologists—and some nonprofessionals—go to purchase shampoos, conditioners, cosmetics, styling tools, extensions, hair colors, and other supplies. If you've gone to beauty school, you'll be familiar with the best brands and products, and aware of what tools beauty professionals need.

If your ambition is to own or manage a beauty supply store, you may want to invest in business education. A solid business education will help you run your business in a professional manner and allow you to avoid unnecessary mistakes that could cost you your dream. Again, this is a career option that will involve more office work than hands-on beauty work.

COSMETOLOGY INSTRUCTORS

Another option is becoming an instructor in a cosmetology school. Perhaps you're the sort of person that "gets things" and can explain them clearly to others. If so, becoming a teacher might be a good fit for you. A good teacher is organized, confident, patient, compassionate, perceptive, and passionate. They can communicate ideas clearly and succinctly. Of course, instructors should have several years of real-world experience under their belts and have a good reputation in the industry. The more respected you are in your field, the more attractive you will be to schools that might want to hire you.

TATTOO ARTIST

Becoming a tattoo artist is another creative career option that might appeal to you. It requires different training and certification than most other beauty work. Tattoo artists need a strong background in drawing. Tattoo artists must also complete training in bloodborne pathogens and often are required to hold a CPR certification. To obtain your license, you must complete an apprenticeship under a licensed tattoo artist as well as any required health or safety classes and pass an exam. Tattoo artists are only allowed to work in dedicated facilities that meet strict health code standards.

Applying tattoos, permanent makeup, or body piercing requires different training from standard cosmetology. There is a greater emphasis on safety and hygiene.

Some beauty schools offer teacher training. Ask your favorite teachers at your beauty school how they got to where they are today. Perhaps you will be able to emulate their career paths. You might consider taking a community class in public speaking to see how comfortable you are talking to a room full of people.

SALON TRAINER AND MANUFACTURER EDUCATOR

There are many ways to pass along your knowledge to other professional cosmetologists. If you like the idea of teaching, but want to stay in the salon environment, you might consider becoming a salon trainer. Many larger salons employ salon trainers. Salon trainers are responsible for training new employees to perform advanced techniques, such as hot new haircuts or new esthetics techniques. As a salon trainer, you will help experienced cosmetology professionals improve their skills so that they can make their clients' lives better.

Or if you prefer something a little different, many beauty supply manufacturers also employ cosmetologists as manufacturer educators. Manufacturer educators travel to salons and train cosmetologists to properly use their products. For instance, a manufacturer educator might travel throughout the northeastern United States introducing hairdressers to a new styling gel. They also give demonstrations at trade shows and conferences.

PREPARING FOR YOUR JOB HUNT

Today's job hunt usually begins online. Sites such as LinkedIn and Indeed are great places to search for a job in your chosen field and location. If you have a particular salon in mind, check out its website. See if there's a section called something like "Careers" or "Come Work for Us." Particularly in the case of chain salons, you might be able to apply right from their website.

You can always walk into your favorite salon with a résumé but be prepared to be told you need to apply online. Your beauty school should also offer career guidance and assistance finding jobs.

Your résumé is an important professional tool. It showcases your skills and job experience for potential employers.

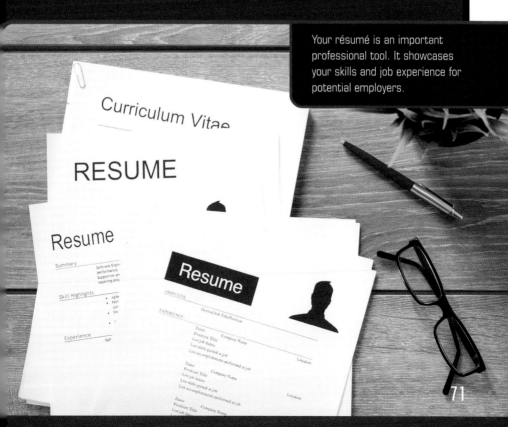

CHAPTER SIX
YOUR FIRST JOB

Cosmetology services are in high demand in today's society. You may recall news stories from the COVID-19 pandemic about people being extremely upset because salons and barber shops were closed for a long time. Styling hair requires close contact—too close for when there was a contagious respiratory disease running wild.

The BLS predicts 89,000 job openings in the hair and makeup industry over the next decade. This growth rate is faster than the national average for other industries. So, once you have your training, how do you get one of those jobs?

BECOMING AN APPRENTICE

Like other hands-on trades, it's possible to get an apprenticeship in cosmetology. As an apprentice hairstylist, you will observe master hairstylists at work and assist them. You'll probably start with the less glamorous tasks—shampooing clients, sweeping up hair, and helping keep clients comfortable. The salon is not only concerned that you learn how to cut, color, and texture according to their methods. It also wants to know that you will fit into the salon's culture—that you can be friendly and professional with clients and a good team member with your salon colleagues.

The pay for these jobs varies from place to place. In many salons, the apprentices earn minimum wage, plus any tips. You may be given the opportunity to give your own haircuts for a lower fee than senior stylists.

Although apprenticeships are often associated with hairdressing, estheticians have assistants and apprentices, too. Research the apprenticeship and internship opportunities in your area. If it works with your school schedule, you might be able to become an apprentice while you're still in cosmetology school. That way, you're more likely to be ready to earn your license and go straight to work when you graduate. Just be careful not to overload your schedule—you're paying for your training, and you need to pass your course to get your license.

It might be possible to work at the same salon where you apprentice. However, this depends on a variety of factors. Before you take an apprentice job

In beauty school, first you'll learn on mannequin heads, then you'll give cuts and styles to your classmates. Finally, you'll work on customers in the school's salon.

at a salon, it's worth asking yourself how well you fit in there. Do you feel comfortable? Have friends? Could you see yourself spending the next few years working there? If you play your cards right, you may earn work experience and get your foot in the door at a great salon—before you even graduate from cosmetology school!

CAREER SERVICES AT COSMETOLOGY SCHOOL

Many places where you'll receive your cosmetology training have job placement services. This includes beauty schools and community colleges. This means the school guides you in your search and, in some cases, actively helps you find a job. In fact, this is one of the main factors you should consider when you are deciding where to go to school. Ask the schools to which you are applying for details on their job placement programs and other career services. Don't be afraid to ask to see job placement statistics or lists of graduates who have found work in prestigious salons.

JOB INTERVIEWS

You've graduated, got your license, and applied for jobs. Now, one has contacted you to ask for an interview. Congratulations! Try not to be nervous. A good interviewer will help you feel comfortable so you can shine.

You want to look nice for the interview—after all, this is for a job in the beauty industry! Business casual is acceptable in most settings—neat pants or a skirt and a nice top or collared shirt. Everything should be clean and neatly pressed. You'll want your hair nicely styled and understated makeup and nails. Go easy on fragrances.

Arrive a few minutes early and give yourself plenty of time to park and get to your interview without rushing and arriving out of breath. Be friendly and polite to anyone you encounter—after all, it may be your interviewer, the business owner, or their best client.

Smile. Make eye contact. Shake hands. Be your awesome self. You've got this!

LOOKING FOR A JOB

No matter what you've seen in the movies, no one graduates and immediately steps right into their dream job with an amazing salary. Even if you've worked as an apprentice and have a job waiting for you, you're still just starting out. Cosmetology school teaches you a lot, but you still have a lot to learn that can only happen out in the real world.

Today, most job ads are posted on websites such as Indeed or LinkedIn. Often these sites have a template for you to create a basic résumé, or you can upload your own. Most word processing programs include templates to create a professional-looking résumé. You'll also need an impressive portfolio, or "book," with photographs of your best work to date. Choose just a few exceptional looks to showcase. The styles you include in your portfolio should give the viewer a taste of your personal style while demonstrating that you can adapt your artistic vision to meet a client's needs.

In addition to applying for advertised positions, there are other job-hunting strategies you can try. Networking is important. Let your friends know that you're in the market for a new job! Ask your friends to tell you if they know about any salons that are looking for employees. Poll your friends and family about their favorite salons and spas. Then contact those places and let them know you are looking for work. Your classmates can be another good source of information—especially any who graduated before you. Consider creating a blog or a website highlighting your work, inspirations, and personal style. This can help you sell yourself to future employers. You can create and print a business card with a QR code to your site relatively inexpensively.

If you are bold, try stopping by a salon or spa you admire to show your résumé and book. Even if they're not hiring, they might be able to tell you about an establishment that is. Or perhaps they'll just keep your résumé on file. Either way, introducing yourself in a friendly and professional manner can't hurt! Always keep a positive attitude. Do use common sense when walking into an establishment to drop off a résumé. Try to go at a quieter time so you won't distract anyone from their business. (Hint: when you Google a business, they often show a graph of busy/quiet times.) Dress neatly and be well groomed. You might be lucky enough to get to speak to someone on the spot.

If all else fails, you can consider getting your foot in the door at a great salon or spa by starting out in a noncreative position, such as receptionist. You'll still be learning about the business and how to talk to clients. In the meantime, keep making yourself more attractive to employers by staying on top of the latest techniques and learning how to do the hottest new procedures.

The receptionist is the first and often the last person a client interacts with, so they need to be welcoming, knowledgeable, and responsible. They'll be booking the client's next appointment and perhaps selling them products.

BEYOND YOUR FIRST JOB

Your first job is as much a learning experience as cosmetology school. You'll learn how to deal with customers, co-workers, and managers. You'll learn that there are no unimportant jobs. Keeping the salon clean and well stocked means that everyone can do their work safely and efficiently. Clients and beauticians alike are happier in a clean, welcoming environment. However, you want to have a plan for your future.

Makeup artists in theaters need to understand how the stage lights affect colors and how to make a dancer or actor's face visible to the back rows.

You have to decide what to do with your training. Do you want to take over your family beauty parlor on Main Street? Go to New York to work in the theater or Los Angeles to work on movies? Or maybe you've noticed a particular service lacking in your hometown and you dream of creating the perfect business to fill that niche. Perhaps you dream of working backstage at fashion shows as a hairstylist.

None of these goals is better or worse—they're what's right for you. Some of them may seem impossible to reach, but the journey of a thousand miles begins with a single step. Brainstorm a series of action steps that will move you closer to your goal, bit by bit. For instance, the most important fashion shows take place during fashion weeks: periods of time when designers show their collections in cities like New York, Los Angeles, and Miami. If you want to work backstage at a fashion show, you'll need to live and work in a city that has a fashion week. The stylists backstage at fashion shows are often hairdressers who work at prestigious salons. So, you'll need to get a job at a respected salon in the city.

Next, break each action step down into even smaller action steps. For instance, before you can get a job at a prestigious salon, you need to know which salons are prestigious. Research the hottest salons in your city and try to meet people who work in them. (Your school's career services can be helpful in making these kinds of contacts.) Then ask your contacts at those salons what they look for in employees. Where did most of their hairstylists go to beauty school? Are there any supplementary classes they recommend? What qualities do these salons look for in an employee?

Attending a trade show is a great way to see what new products and techniques are available. You can talk to people and get new career ideas.

Most job hunting and networking is done online.

If you can't even imagine what action steps might lead you toward your goal, get on the web and find some people who have already achieved your career goal. If they're well established in the industry, they most likely they have a website, Facebook page, or other social media. Contact them politely and respectfully and ask them if they would be willing to talk to you about how they got where they are. If you find people who are willing to answer some of your questions, you might ask: Did they go to an excellent beauty school? Which one? Did they gain some valuable experience in high school? Do they have any advice for aspiring cosmetologists? Ask yourself how you might follow the career path that they forged.

You can learn more about how to fulfill your beauty industry goals by reading trade magazines such as *American Salon* and *Modern Salon*. Consider attending beauty conventions and trade shows. Talk with any professionals you meet. Connect with cosmetologists in your area and ask them to share their thoughts about how you might build a career.

It's good to have a career goal and a plan to get there. It's also OK if that goal or plan changes. Sometimes things look much better on paper than they are in real life. Theater, film, and high fashion can be incredibly rewarding careers. They're also highly stressful and competitive and take a lot of work to achieve. The cost of living in a major theater or fashion city is astronomical.

You may eventually decide you'd be happier working in a theater in a smaller city, or teaching, or relocating to a spa or resort in a cool vacation spot. Maybe you'd like to travel to clients instead of working in a salon. The possibilities are endless.

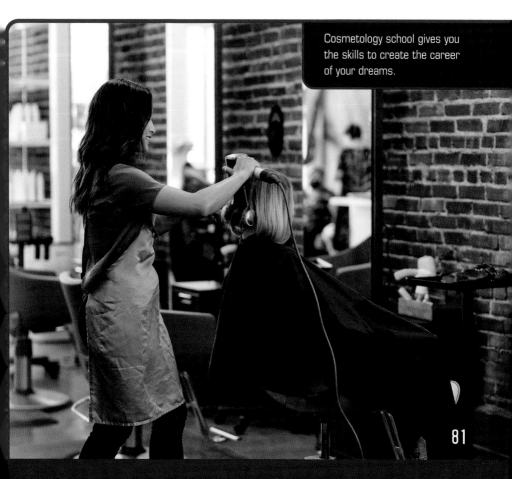

Cosmetology school gives you the skills to create the career of your dreams.

81

10 GREAT QUESTIONS TO ASK A COSMETOLOGIST

Here are some questions you can ask a cosmetologist. Try to speak to people with different specialties who work in different places if you can. This will give you a better overview of the profession.

1 Did you attend cosmetology school or some other type of training?
2 Why did you choose it?
3 Did you take any additional special classes or certifications?
4 There are a lot of beauty magazines and blogs. Which ones do you recommend?
5 What's your dream career?
6 What can I do to prepare for a career in cosmetology while I'm still in high school?
7 Is this the only setting you've worked in?
8 Do you own your own business?
9 Do you belong to any professional organizations?
10 Is there anything you wish someone had told you when you first considered this career?

What other questions can you think of?

Talk to your barber or hairdresser about why they chose their career. Who knows—maybe when you're ready for an apprenticeship, they'll be happy to talk to you again.

GLOSSARY

accredited: Officially recognized as meeting the quality standards of an accrediting agency for curriculum, instruction, facilities, etc.

apprentice: A junior artisan or craftsperson who learns from a more experienced colleague, while working for low wages in exchange for hands-on training in a trade.

barber: A personal appearance worker who specializes in cutting men's hair and shaving facial hair.

callus: A part of the skin that has become harder and thicker than the skin surrounding it.

chemical peel: A beauty treatment that uses chemicals to peel a layer of dead skin away from the face, leaving younger and smoother skin behind.

corrective makeup: Makeup meant to camouflage certain facial features or blemishes. Corrective makeup can be used to slim a face, mask a scar, and make features look more balanced.

cowlick: A section of hair that grows in a different direction or pattern than the hair surrounding it.

cuticle: The thick skin lining the sides and bases of the fingernails and toenails.

dandruff: Flakes of dead skin that are sometimes found in hair.

diplomatic: Able to deal with sensitive people and situations without causing offense.

exfoliation: The process of washing or treating the surface of the skin with a cosmetic preparation to remove dead skin cells, revealing the healthy skin beneath.

financial aid: Grants, scholarships, or loans intended to help a student pay for his or her education. Financial aid may be provided by a school, an outside organization, or the government.

hair follicle: A small cavity in the skin where an individual hair is rooted. Each hair grows from a follicle.

head lice: Tiny parasitic insects that live in hair and feed on blood through the scalp.

mannequin head: A fake head with hair that is used by cosmetology students to practice techniques for cutting, styling, curling, and perming hair.

portfolio: A set of drawings, paintings, or photographs that are presented together in a folder.

solvent: A liquid substance that is used to dissolve another substance.

sterilization: The process of killing any microscopic organisms such as bacteria, fungi, or viruses. Cosmetologists sterilize their equipment so that they will not unwittingly pass infectious diseases and pests between clients.

updo: A hairstyle that sweeps the hair up, away from the face and neck, instead of letting it hang loose. Updos are often used for formal occasions like weddings.

vocational high school: A high school that aims to give its graduates a firm grounding in a vocation, or trade, so that they will be ready to go to work soon after graduating.

FOR MORE INFORMATION

ALLIED BEAUTY ASSOCIATION
BOX 30068 Cityside Postal Outlet
Mississauga, ON
Canada
(905) 568-0158
Website: www.abacanada.com
Facebook and Instagram: @ABACanada
The ABA represents Canadian beauty professionals.

AMERICAN ASSOCIATION OF COSMETOLOGY SCHOOLS (AACS)
20 F Street, N.W.
Suite 700
Washington, D.C. 20001
(202) 963-5730
Website: www.beautyschools.org
Facebook: @AmericanAssociationOfCosmetologySchools
Instagram: @aacschools
AACS is an organization that champions cosmetology education. They provide resources for students, and lobby in Washington for legislation pertinent to the industry.

AMERICAN BARBER ASSOCIATION
P.O. Box 11661
Shorewood, WI 53211
(929) 399-6233
Website: www.americanbarber.org
Facebook: @BarberUSA
Instagram: @barbersusa
ABA is a leading source of information and education for the barber industry.

ASSOCIATED HAIR PROFESSIONALS
25188 Genesee Trail Road
Suite 200
Golden, CO 80401
(800) 575-4642
Website: www.associatedhairprofessionals.com
Facebook and Instagram: @ahphair
AHP is a professional organization for hairstylists and barbers. They offer educational, professional, and community support for hair professionals.

BEAUTYCOUNCIL
P.O. Box 16002
North Vancouver, BC V7J 3S9
Canada
(604) 871-0222
Website: www.beautycouncil.ca
BeautyCouncil is a community of salon, spa, and barber professionals located in western Canada.

INTERNATIONAL ALLIANCE OF THEATRICAL STAGE EMPLOYEES
Moving Picture Technicians, Artists and Allied Crafts of the United States, Its Territories and Canada
207 W. 25th St, 4th Fl.
New York, NY 10001
(212) 730-1770
Website: iatse.net
Facebook and Instagram: @iatse
IATSE is the labor union that represents stylists and makeup artists who work in the entertainment industry.

MADAM C.J. WALKER
Website: madamcjwalker.com
The official website of Madam C. J. Walker contains media and biographical information.

MILADY
5 Maxwell Dr.
Clifton Park, NY 12065
(866) 848-5143
Website: www.milady.com
Milady publishes one of the most widely used cosmetology textbooks and curriculums.

NATIONAL ASSOCIATION OF BARBER BOARDS OF AMERICA
9252 San Jose Blvd. #3703
Jacksonville, FL 32257
(888) 338-0101
Website: nationalbarberboards.com
The National Association of Barber Boards of America is an organization dedicated to maintaining professional standards and policies in the barbering industry.

PIVOT POINT
8725 W. Higgins Road
Suite 700
Chicago, IL 60631
(847) 866-0500
Website: www.pivot-point.com
Facebook: @PivotPointInternational
Instagram: @pivotpointintl
Pivot Point publishes one of the most widely used cosmetology textbooks, as well as mannequins and hairstyling tools.

PROFESSIONAL BEAUTY ASSOCIATION
7755 E. Gray Road
Scottsdale, AZ 85260
(480) 281-0424
Website: www.probeauty.org
Facebook: @professionalbeautyassociation
Instagram: @probeautyassoc
PBA is a trade organization that represents all aspects of the beauty industry.

VOGUE
1 World Trade Center
New York, NY 10007
(800) 234-2347
Website: www.vogue.com/magazine
Facebook: @Vogue
Instagram: @voguemagazine
Vogue is generally considered the pinnacle of the fashion magazine industry. Working for the magazine is the ultimate goal of many print stylists.

FOR FURTHER READING

Ali, Hana. *How to Become a Professional Makeup Artist: Your Guide to a Successful Start in the Beauty Industry*. Independently published, 2020.

Daego, Nailah. *Cosmetology State Board Written Practice Exam Book with 5 Mock Exams and 550 Practice Questions*. Independently published, 2023.

Enoch, Joshua. *From Barber to a Business: The Simple Guide to Becoming a Successful Barber*. Independently published, 2021.

Freedman, Jeri. *Makeup and Styling in TV and Film*. New York, NY: Cavendish Square, 2019.

Javor, Alexandra. *Hairstyling Kit Checklist: Pack Your Mobile Kit Efficiently for Weddings & Other Events*. Independently published, 2023.

Joseph, Donnie. *The Habits of a Six-Figure Barber: Unlock Your Potential Behind the Chair.* Independently published, 2022.

Milady. *Milady's Standard Cosmetology 14th Edition.* Clifton Park, NY: Cengage Learning, 2021.

Stronach, Julia. *Business for Makeup Artists: HOW TO GROW YOUR MAKEUP BUSINESS FAST!* Independently published, 2020.

Sutcliffe, Hank. *All About the Esthetics Business: The Ultimate Guide to Maximize Your Income as an Esthetician: Esthetician Salary.* Independently published, 2021.

Syrewicz, Connor. *Massage Therapist: Providing Relief & Relaxation.* Philadelphia, PA: Mason Crest, 2020.

INDEX

A

aesthetics/esthetics, 13–14, 34–47, 60–62, 73
apprenticeship, 72–73

B

barber, 13, 22, 59
Bureau of Labor Statistics (U.S.), 8, 72
business skills/management, 66–68

C

cosmetic surgery, 62
creativity, 10–11, 14, 25, 27, 65

E

education
    college, 12, 15–16, 18, 68, 74
    cosmetology school, 13–19, 27–29, 31,
        44, 48, 52, 58, 70–71, 73–75, 77
    cost, 13, 15–20, 73
    high school, 12–14, 63
    massage school, 63
    nail technology school, 56–57
    vocational, 12
ethnicity/race, 14, 28–29

H

hair dye, 14, 30–31, 66
hair removal, 13–14, 40–41, 43, 60–61
hair styling, 14, 25–28, 54–55, 57
health, 22–23, 35–38, 40, 48, 50, 62
history, 4–8

I

International Alliance of Theatrical Stage
        Employees, Moving Picture Technicians,
        Artists and Allied Crafts of the United
        States, Its Territories and Canada, 46
internship, 73

J

job interview, 74–75
job prospects/search, 8, 17, 42, 71–82
Joyner, Marjorie Stewart, 29

L

licensing/certification, 12, 15–16, 20, 41, 43,
        56–57, 61–63, 65, 69

S

T

W

ABOUT THE AUTHOR

KATHLEEN A. KLATTE is the author of many nonfiction books for children and teens. Topics range from animals and nature to constitutional law to unusual career choices. She lives in New York with one cat and far too many books and Legos.

PHOTO CREDITS